AWESOME LOGIC PUZZLES FOR KIDS

60 Clever Brain Games and Puzzles

AWESOME LOGIC PUZZLES

FOR KIDS

Shametria Routt Banks

ROCKRIDGE
PRESS

Thanks to my mom for always being my biggest cheerleader and for helping make this book come to life. I would also like to thank my husband, Derek, and my family for their continued love and support. Finally, I'm grateful to Dr. Trena Wilkerson for shaping the way I teach math.

Interior and Cover Designer: Angie Chiu
Art Producer: Hannah Dickerson
Editor: Alyson Penn
Production Editor: Nora Milman
Production Manager: Holly Haydash

Illustrations © 2021 Collaborate Agency
Author photo courtesy of The AWE Studio, 2020

Paperback ISBN: 978-1-64876-711-1
R0

CONTENTS

A NOTE TO AWESOME KIDS

s a little girl, I loved solving puzzles! I was curious about the world around me and asked lots of questions about how things worked. I loved solving math problems, because they always had an answer. I was proud of myself after I solved a problem or completed a puzzle.

When I started teaching almost 20 years ago, I decided to share my love of math, brain teasers, and puzzles with my students. We started every lesson with a math challenge—my students loved them!

In the first chapter of this book, you will explore patterns, which are designs that repeat (sometimes in shapes, colors, lines, symbols, numbers, letters, words, or a combination of those things). From patterns on animals to patterns on flowers, you can find patterns everywhere in the world around you. For each new puzzle, you will use your thinking skills to look for the part of the picture that repeats and then add to the pattern.

The next chapter is all about sequences. A **sequence** is a list of things in order. You can spot a sequence when you see something that looks like a pattern, but it changes a little for each new piece of the pattern. In this chapter, you will use your thinking skills to look for the part of each picture that is different and then decide what comes next.

Chapter 3 will build your vocabulary skills through analogies, which are comparisons between two things. Solving analogies grows your brain and helps you see how two things are related. After you examine the first two items, you will use the relationship between them to complete the second pair of items.

In the fourth chapter, you will test your visual thinking skills with **matchstick puzzles**. To solve these puzzles, you will use critical thinking to move matchsticks in your head and create new pictures. Learning to solve puzzles like this will strengthen your geometry and critical thinking skills.

In chapter 5, you will solve **logic puzzles**. Using your detective skills, you will read a set of clues and complete a chart to help you narrow down the choices and find the solution.

The last chapter is about strengthening your **reasoning skills**. You will have to think like a scientist to solve word problems and number-logic puzzles, complete logic sentences, and decide which picture is not like the others.

Every chapter has 10 puzzles. The first puzzles in each chapter are the easiest so you can practice and get the hang of them, but each new puzzle is a little harder than the one before it. Don't worry, though; you have more than enough brainpower to solve the puzzles. Plus, the last two puzzles in each chapter have a hint if you need a little help.

Ready to get started? You can tackle the book in any way you want. You can start at the beginning or start with your favorite puzzle—your choice. The main goals are to have fun, stretch your thinking, and challenge your family and friends. You've got this!

CHAPTER I

PATTERNS IN OUR WORLD

INTRODUCTION

A pattern is something that repeats or looks the same over and over. When you learn to see patterns, you find them all around you. A blanket or the tiles on the floor have patterns made with squares, triangles, or circles. Nature is full of patterns, too, like the spots on a leopard or the shapes in a honeycomb where bees store honey.

How can you spot a pattern? Look at each part of the picture. Ask yourself how the picture changes. Can you guess what comes next?

Here's an example:

First, we see a card with a red heart. Then, we see two black clubs and another red heart. If we follow the pattern, then two black clubs will come next.

It's your turn! Each pattern in this chapter gets a little harder than the one before. Use the hints to help you with the last two patterns. You can do it!

DOUBLE DOTS

Wyatt used a set of dice to make the patterns below. Which dice come next? For each of the blank dice, draw the number of dots and the correct color.

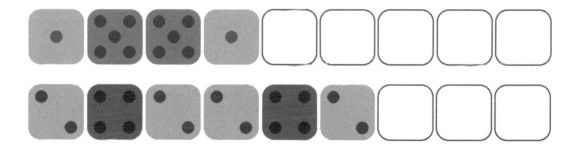

RIDDLE ME THIS! What is the saddest fruit?

MAKING PATTERNS WITH PAWNS

Truman used game pawns from a board game to make these patterns. What color pawns come next? Color the blank pawns to complete each pattern.

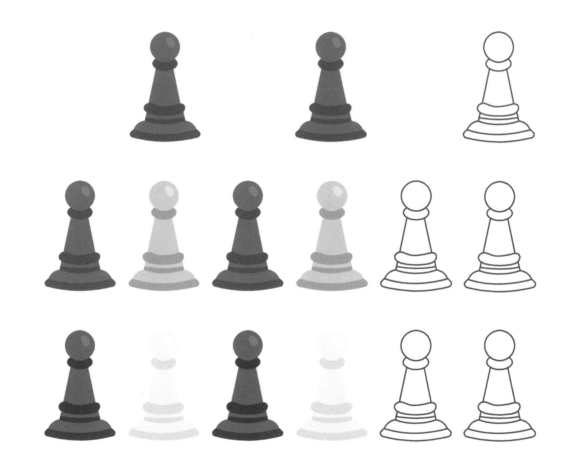

RIDDLE ME THIS! Which fruit can be used to sip a drink?

FUN WITH SPINNERS

Sajan created a pattern with a set of spinners. Which two spinners come next? Draw and color the next two blank spinners.

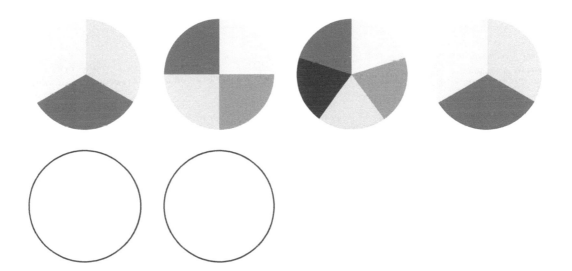

RIDDLE ME THIS! Which vegetable has ears but can't hear?

Patterns in Our World   5

PLAYING CARD PATTERNS

Annaliese created this pattern using a set of playing cards.
What patterns do you see? Use the space below to describe the
patterns you see in numbers, colors, and shapes on the cards.
Then describe the card that comes next.

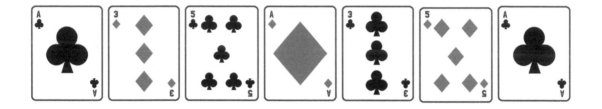

_____

_____

_____

_____

_____

RIDDLE ME THIS! Which vegetable do people cry over?

READY, SET, TIC-TAC-TOE

Kailey created this pattern after playing tic-tac-toe with her little brother. What comes next? Draw and color the next two parts of the pattern.

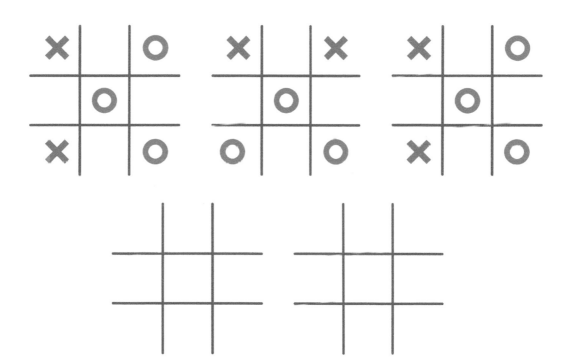

RIDDLE ME THIS! Which fruit cannot be alone?

DICEY PATTERNS

Paris created this pattern with a set of dice. What comes next?
Draw and color the next four parts of the dice pattern.

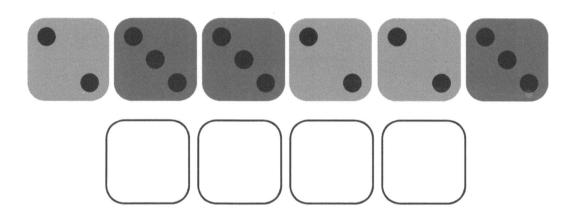

RIDDLE ME THIS! Which vegetable never wins a competition?

DOMINO PATTERNS

Anson created this pattern with a set of dominoes. What comes next? Draw and color the next four dominoes in the pattern.

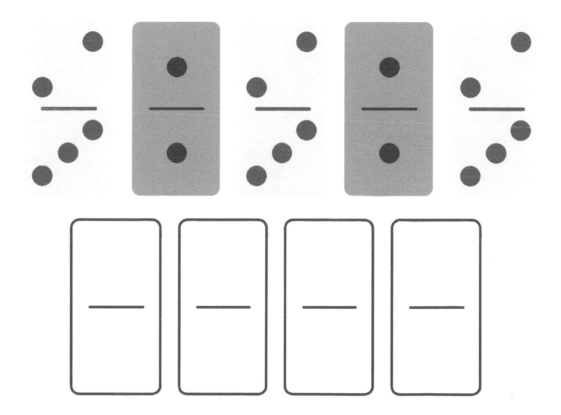

RIDDLE ME THIS! Which fruit makes people go crazy?

SPINNING SPINNERS

Wyatt created a pattern with a set of spinners. Which three spinners come next? Draw and color the next three spinners.

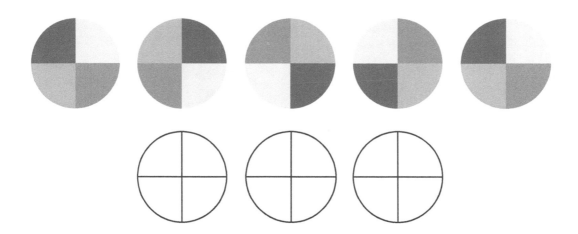

RIDDLE ME THIS! What is a bee's favorite fruit?

FUN WITH DOTS AND DICE

Ramitha used a set of dice to make these patterns. Fill in the correct color and draw the correct number of dots in the blank dice below to complete the patterns.

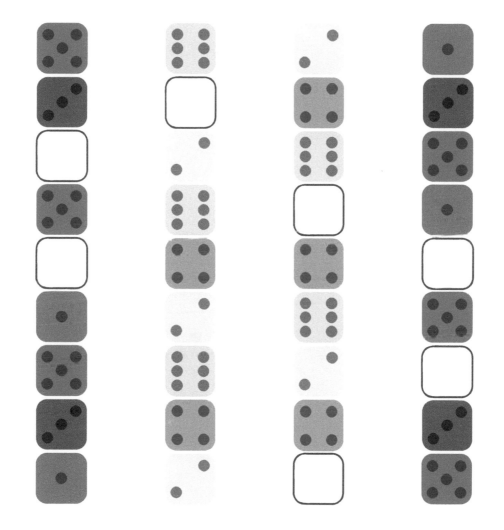

RIDDLE ME THIS!

Which fruit is most like a chicken?

✳ Hint: Look at the sequences of three dice in each column. What do you notice?

SEEING SPOTS

Anson created this pattern with a set of dominoes. Fill in the correct color and draw the correct number of dots on the missing dominoes to complete the pattern.

✳ **Hint:** Look at the numbers on each set of two dominoes. What do you notice?

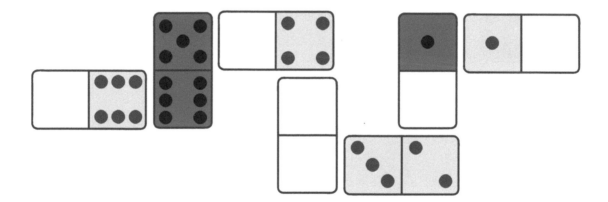

RIDDLE ME THIS! Which vegetable has the best animal collection?

CHAPTER 2

FOLLOW THAT SEQUENCE

INTRODUCTION

A **sequence** is a list of things in order. When you look
at a sequence, you see the same thing happen over
and over with a small change each time. Sequences
are patterns we see around us, like the number of
petals on a flower, spirals in a pine cone, or seeds in
a sunflower. When you see sequences in nature, you'll
notice similar ones.

How can you spot sequences? Ask yourself how
each new picture changes. Can you guess what
comes next?

Here's an example:

Picture 1 **Picture 2** **Picture 3**

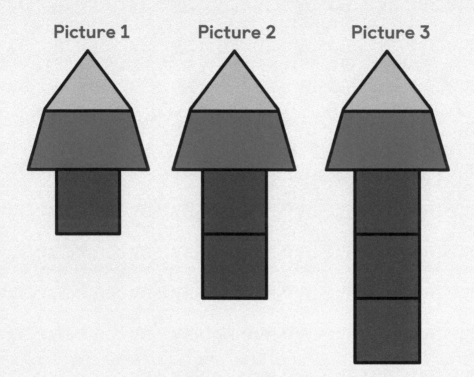

First, we see a treetop with one trunk square. The next picture is a treetop and two squares. The third is a treetop and three squares. If we follow the pattern, we know the next picture has a treetop and four squares.

It's your turn! Each sequence in this chapter gets a little harder than the one before. Use the hints to help you with the last two sequences. You've got this!

LEMONADE STAND

In these pictures, what happens first? Second? Third? Fourth? Write the numbers 1, 2, 3, and 4 on the lines below the pictures to show the correct order of the steps to make lemonade.

RIDDLE ME THIS! What has two legs and catches flies?

RAINY WEATHER

In these pictures, what happens first? Second? Third? Fourth? Write the numbers 1, 2, 3, and 4 on the lines below the pictures to show the correct order of how the weather changes.

_____

_____

_____

_____

RIDDLE ME THIS!

What do you get when you cross a pig and a basketball player?

SKIP COUNTING

Look at the following sequence. Write the missing numbers on the T-shirts to complete the sequence.

1. 3
2. 9
3.
4. 21
5.

RIDDLE ME THIS! Which kind of cat is the best at bowling?

NUMBER SEQUENCES

Look at the following sequence. Write the missing numbers on the T-shirts to complete the sequence.

1. 16

2.

3. 32

4. 40

5.

RIDDLE ME THIS! What soccer position does a ghost play?

HUNDREDS CHART PICTURES

Use what you know about the hundreds chart to fill in the empty boxes on the puzzle piece on this page. Use the example to help you see the number sequences on a hundreds chart and how to complete the puzzle.

* Example of a Completed Hundreds Chart

RIDDLE ME THIS! What do a baseball team and cupcakes have in common?

FIND THE MISSING NUMBERS

Use what you know about the hundreds chart to fill in the empty boxes on the puzzle piece below. Use the example on the previous page to help you.

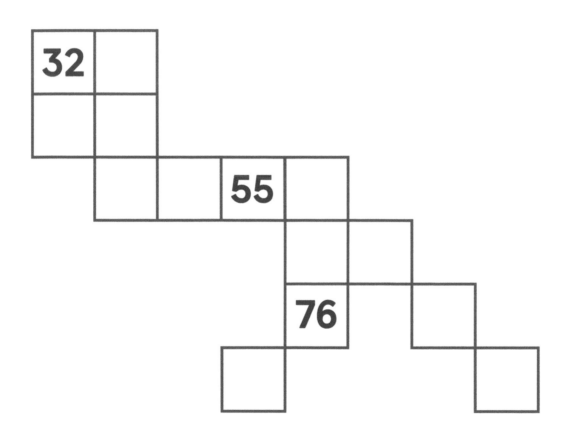

RIDDLE ME THIS! What animal makes the best baseball player?

INTERSECTING SQUARES

Look at the sequence of pictures below. Draw the next two pictures in the sequence.

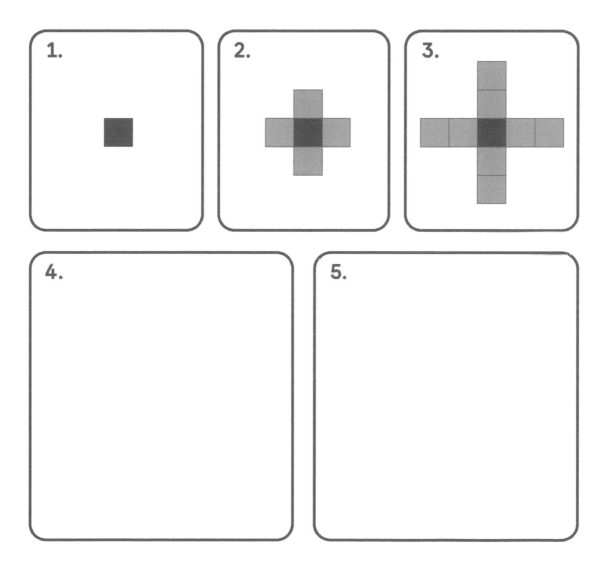

1.

2.

3.

4.

5.

RIDDLE ME THIS! Why did the football coach yell at the cashier?

TRICKY TRIANGLES

Look at the sequence of pictures below. Draw the next two pictures in the sequence.

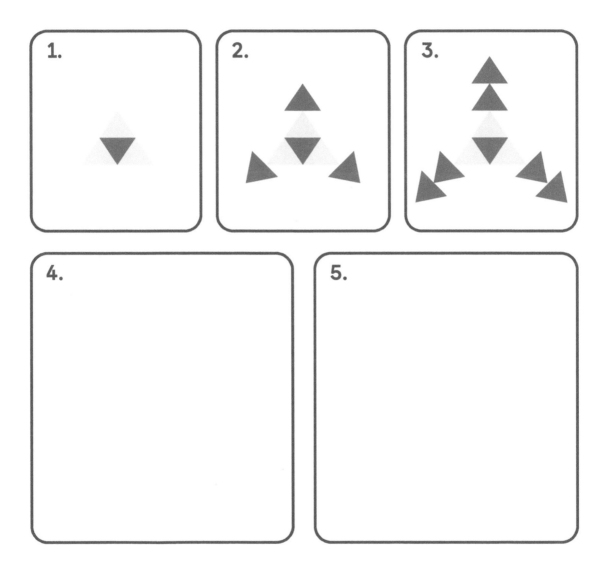

1.

2.

3.

4.

5.

RIDDLE ME THIS! What do basketball players do to stay cool during a game?

SQUARE STAIRCASES

Look at the sequence of pictures below. Draw the next two pictures in the sequence.

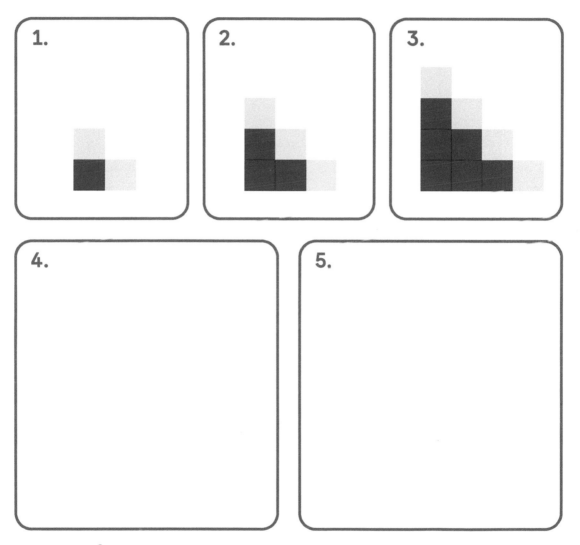

1.

2.

3.

4.

5.

❋ **Hint:** How does one picture look different from the one that comes before it? What do you notice about the bottom row of purple squares?

RIDDLE ME THIS! What kind of sport uses a ball that has feet but no hands?

GROWING GARDENS

Look at the sequence of pictures below. Draw the next two pictures in the sequence.

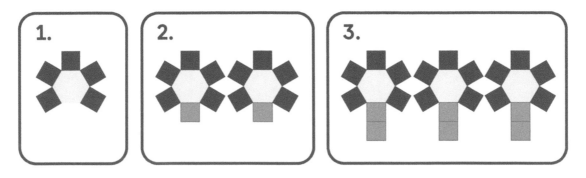

1.

2.

3.

4.

5.

🌸 Hint: How do the flowers and stems change? Do the changes match the picture number?

RIDDLE ME THIS! What is the hardest thing for a runner to catch?

CHAPTER 3

APPLES TO ORANGES AND OTHER ANALOGIES

INTRODUCTION

An analogy is a comparison between two items. Understanding analogies will increase the number of words you know and build your thinking skills. For example, if you can figure out how the first pair of objects or group of objects is related, then you will know how the second group is related.

How can you spot an analogy? Ask yourself how the first two items are related. Then think about two things with the same relationship.

Here's an example:

If you were going to describe the images above in words, you might say it this way:

Green circle is to green cylinder as purple square is to purple _____ .

We can see the top and bottom of the cylinder are circles, so the missing image must have a top and bottom that are squares. A cube has squares on the top and bottom, so that is the missing picture.

If you were going to describe the images above in words, you might say it this way:

Green circle is to green cylinder as purple square is to purple <u>cube</u>.

Now it's your turn! Each set of analogies in this chapter gets a little harder than the ones before. Use the hints to help you with the last two sets. Time to build your brainpower!

SPORTS SPECTACULAR

In the blank space, draw or write the sport or object that completes the analogy.

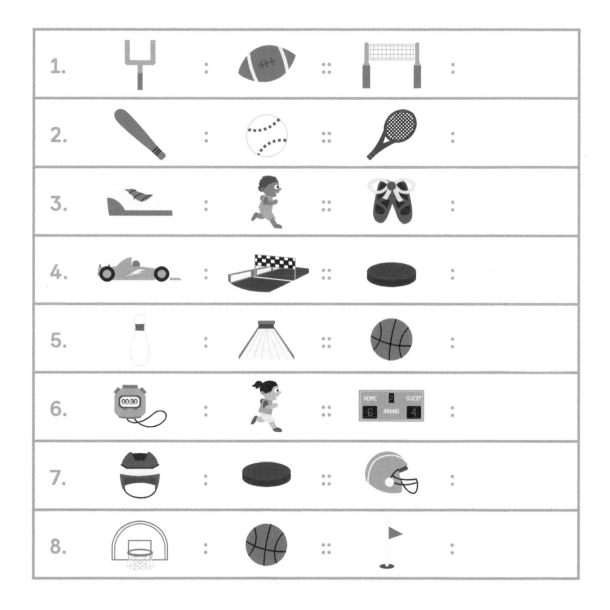

1. [goalpost] : [football] :: [volleyball net] : _____

2. [baseball bat] : [baseball] :: [tennis racket] : _____

3. [ski jump] : [runner] :: [ballet shoes] : _____

4. [race car] : [finish line] :: [hockey puck] : _____

5. [bowling pin] : [bowling lane] :: [basketball] : _____

6. [stopwatch] : [runner] :: [scoreboard] : _____

7. [catcher's mask] : [hockey puck] :: [football helmet] : _____

8. [basketball hoop] : [basketball] :: [golf flag] : _____

RIDDLE ME THIS! Which animal was caught cheating in school?

WHERE DO I BELONG?

Write the word in the blank space that completes the analogy.

1. carrot : vegetable :: **apple** : _____

2. polar bear : mammal :: **seagull** : _____

3. shark : fish :: **butterfly** : _____

4. cereal : breakfast :: **ice cream** : _____

5. tree : forest :: **cactus** : _____

6. ant : insect :: **crocodile** : _____

7. calculator : math :: **microscope** : _____

8. paintbrush : art :: **drums** : _____

RIDDLE ME THIS! Why do frogs have more lives than cats?

WHAT'S THE RULE?

Write the number in the blank space that completes the analogy.

1.	15 : 30	::	20 : 40
2.	24 : 12	::	32 : _____
3.	25 : 50	::	30 : _____
4.	40 : 80	::	50 : _____
5.	10 : 5	::	16 : _____
6.	90 : 45	::	100 : _____
7.	50 : 100	::	75 : _____
8.	300 : 150	::	200 : _____

✳ **Hint:** Think about doubles and halves.

RIDDLE ME THIS! How do bees travel to school?

SEEING MULTIPLES

Write the number in the blank space that completes the analogy.

1.	21 : 7	::	30 : 10	
2.	20 : 5	::	36 : _____	
3.	4 : 20	::	16 : _____	
4.	30 : 6	::	55 : _____	
5.	9 : 54	::	12 : _____	
6.	48 : 8	::	60 : _____	
7.	8 : 56	::	7 : _____	
8.	35 : 5	::	49 : _____	

✳ **Hint:** Use multiplication and division facts to help you.

RIDDLE ME THIS! What happened after a lion swallowed a clown?

CHAPTER 4

MOVING MATCHSTICKS

INTRODUCTION

A matchstick puzzle is a picture made with matchsticks. Working on matchstick puzzles is a fun way to stretch your brain, make math visual, and think about things in three dimensions. Mastering matchstick puzzles will help you better understand how to move and change 3D shapes and objects in your head.

How do you solve a matchstick puzzle? Move the matchsticks around in your head or use pretzels or toothpicks to help you see how adding or removing matchsticks changes the picture.

Here's an example:

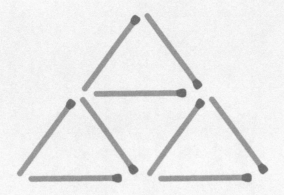

Right now, we see four triangles. Try moving two matchsticks in the middle to make one big triangle and one triangle in the corner of the big triangle. Do you see it?

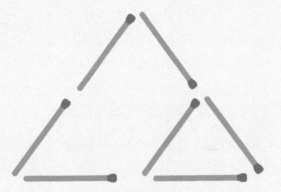

Now it's your turn! Each set of matchstick puzzles in this chapter gets a little harder than the one before. Use the hints to help you with the last two puzzles. Let's stretch your thinking!

MATCHSTICK HOUSES

Remove one matchstick to create a **pentagon**, a shape that has five sides.

Remove one matchstick to create a trapezoid and two squares.

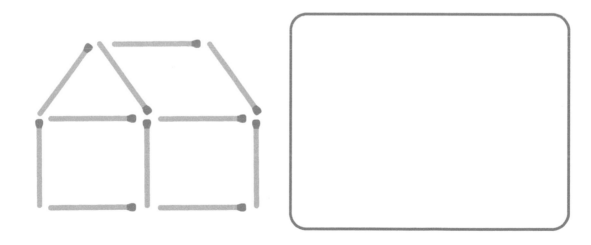

RIDDLE ME THIS! Why did Nose decide to skip school today?

MORE OR LESS

Remove one matchstick to make a number that is 100 less than the number below.

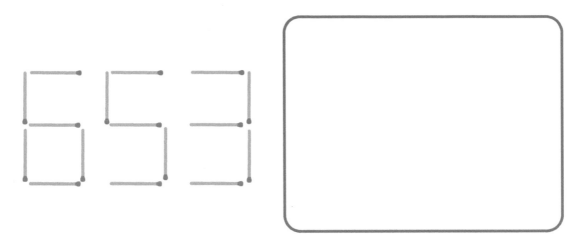

Remove one matchstick to make a number that is 100 more than the number below.

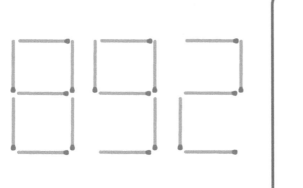

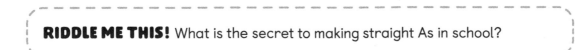
RIDDLE ME THIS! What is the secret to making straight As in school?

STARTING WITH SQUARES

Move one matchstick to create an uppercase letter of the alphabet.

Move one matchstick to create a football goal post.

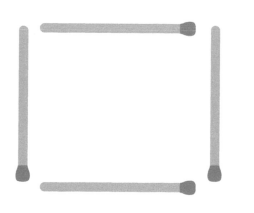

RIDDLE ME THIS! How did the music teacher get locked out of his classroom?

NINE MORE OR LESS

Move one matchstick to make a number that is nine less than the number below.

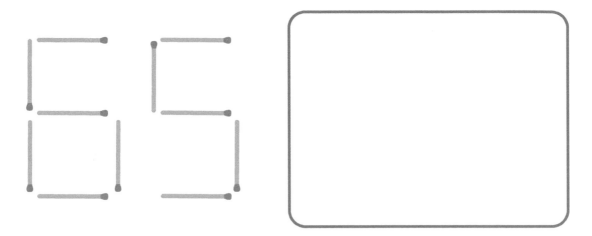

Move one matchstick to make a number that is nine more than the number below.

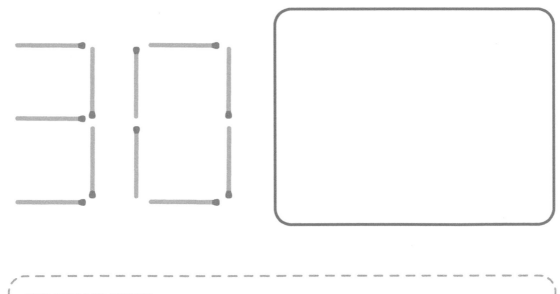

TRANSFORMING TRIANGLES

Move two matchsticks to create a trapezoid and a triangle.

Move two matchsticks to create four triangles.

RIDDLE ME THIS! What kind of bait do librarians use to catch fish?

MATCHSTICK EQUALITIES

Move two matchsticks to create a true statement. You may need to create different numbers and use a different sign to do this.

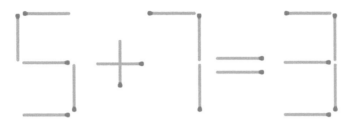

Move two matchsticks to create a true statement. You may need to create different numbers and use a different sign to do this.

SMALLEST TO LARGEST

Move three matchsticks to make the smallest possible number with these three digits.

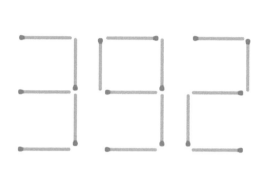 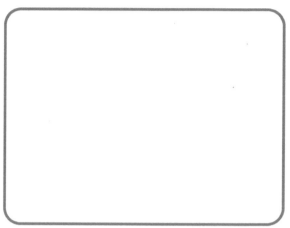

Move three matchsticks to make the largest possible number with these three digits.

 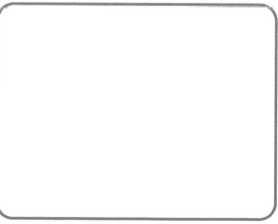

RIDDLE ME THIS! Why did the teacher put on her sunglasses?

BALANCING EQUATIONS

Move two matchsticks to balance the equation, by making both sides of the equation equal 6.

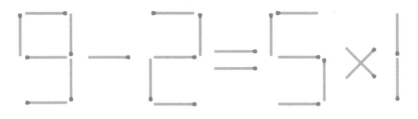

$$9 - 2 = 5 \times 1$$

Move two matchsticks to balance the equation, by making both sides of the equation equal 15.

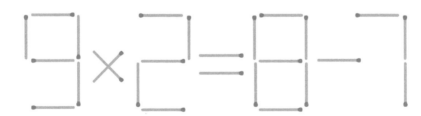

$$9 \times 2 = 8 - 7$$

RIDDLE ME THIS! Why did the kitchen timer in the cafeteria run so slow?

SEEING SQUARES

Remove two matchsticks to leave just two squares. The squares do not have to be the same size.

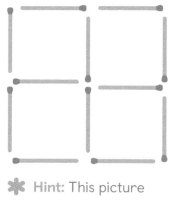

🌻 Hint: This picture shows five squares.

Remove eight matchsticks to leave just six squares. The squares do not have to be the same size.

🌻 Hint: Small squares can be combined to make a larger square.

RIDDLE ME THIS! What math tool is king of the classroom?

MAKING WORDS

Move two matchsticks and remove one matchstick to spell out the smallest odd number as a word.

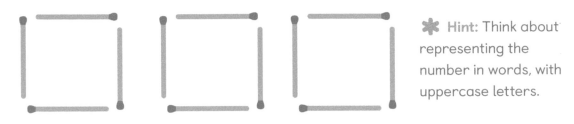

✳ Hint: Think about representing the number in words, with uppercase letters.

Move three matchsticks and remove three matchsticks to spell out the smallest two-digit number as a word.

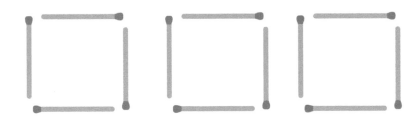

✳ Hint: Think about representing the number in words, with uppercase letters.

RIDDLE ME THIS! What is an owl's favorite class at school?

CHAPTER 5

FOR THE LOVE OF LOGIC

INTRODUCTION

A logic puzzle uses clues to find a solution. Logic puzzles help build important thinking skills. Solving them will help you learn to use clues to arrive at a conclusion, like a detective.

To solve a logic puzzle, read the clues and use checks to show when two things match and Xs to show when they don't match.

Here's an example:

Four friends went to the fall carnival together. Each person chose a different favorite activity. Use the clues to determine each friend's favorite activity. In the chart below, use a check for the favorite activity and Xs for the rest.

1. Andrew enjoys activities with water but doesn't like competition.

2. Bertha is a softball player and really enjoys being the pitcher.

3. Carlina gets carsick easily.

	Duck Pond	Musical Chairs	Hayride	Dunking Booth
Andrew	✔	✘	✘	✘
Bertha	✘	✘	✘	✔
Carlina	✘	✔	✘	✘
DeWayne	✘	✘	✔	✘

Based on the clues, we know Andrew likes water activities, like the duck pond and dunking booth. However, he doesn't like competition, which rules out the dunking booth, so we know Andrew chose the duck pond. We know Bertha likes pitching, which you do at the dunking booth, so she chose the dunking booth. Because Carlina gets carsick, she doesn't like hayrides, so we know she must have chosen musical chairs. That means DeWayne chose the hayride.

It's your turn! Each logic puzzle gets a little harder than the one before. Use the hints to help you with the last two. Let's go, supersleuth!

A TRIP TO THE ZOO

Angelo and his friends visited the zoo. Each person bought a different stuffed animal in the gift shop. Use the clues below to figure out the animal each friend bought. In the chart below, use a check for the chosen animal and Xs for the rest.

1. Collin's favorite animal lives in a cold climate.

2. Angelo's favorite animal is a big cat that lives in Africa and Asia.

3. Brooke's favorite animal is a bird that cannot fly and swims in cold ocean water.

4. Donetta's favorite animal is a bird that likes warm weather.

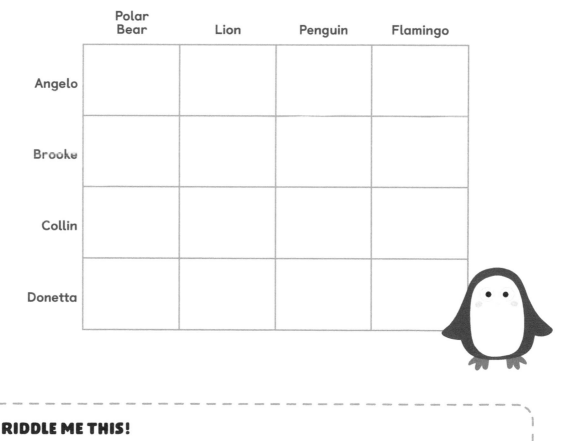

	Polar Bear	Lion	Penguin	Flamingo
Angelo				
Brooke				
Collin				
Donetta				

RIDDLE ME THIS!
What do we call a circus performer who can see in the dark?

TOY DEPARTMENT

The toy department at the local store sells eight different stuffed animals. The bottom shelf has penguins, polar bears, seals, and dolphins. The top shelf has cheetahs, giraffes, lions, and zebras. Use the clues to determine the placement of the animals on the top shelf. In the chart below, use a check for the chosen animal's placement and Xs for the rest.

1. The giraffes are not on either end of the shelf.

2. The cheetahs are next to the lions.

3. The lions are not on either end of the shelf.

4. The zebras are on the far left.

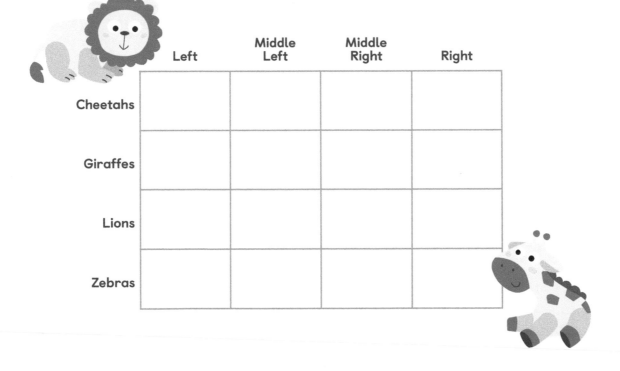

	Left	Middle Left	Middle Right	Right
Cheetahs				
Giraffes				
Lions				
Zebras				

RIDDLE ME THIS! What happened to the human cannonball?

THE REPTILE HOUSE

The reptile house is a circular building at the zoo that includes turtles, iguanas, snakes, a Komodo dragon, and crocodiles. Use the clues to determine the order of the animal enclosures starting at the entrance. In the chart below, use a check for the chosen animal's placement and Xs for the rest.

1. The crocodiles are not in the center enclosure.

2. The snakes and the turtles have enclosures on the far sides.

3. The iguanas are not on the right side of the gallery.

4. The Komodo dragon is on the left side of the crocodiles.

5. The turtles are to the left of the snakes.

	Left Side	Middle Left	Center	Middle Right	Right Side
Turtles					
Iguanas					
Snakes					
Komodo Dragon					
Crocodiles					

RIDDLE ME THIS! What happened when the clown made the magician mad?

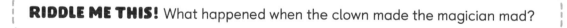

GO-KART RACES

Arnav, Bobby, Cam, and Diego are in line waiting for their turn to ride the go-karts. When it is their turn to enter the track, each boy races to a car painted in his favorite color. Use the clues to determine which color car (red, yellow, green, or blue) each boy chose. In the chart below, use a check for the favorite color and Xs for the rest.

1. Arnav chose the yellow or green car.

2. Bobby chose the color car that begins with the same letter as his name.

3. Cam's favorite colors are red and green.

4. Diego's grandfather bought him a toy fire truck for his birthday because it was his favorite color.

	Red	Yellow	Green	Blue
Arnav				
Bobby				
Cam				
Diego				

RIDDLE ME THIS!
What do you get when you call a clown three times?

HAUNTED MANSION

Alma, Bettina, Camila, and Danielle waited in line to visit the drama club's haunted mansion at the local high school for more than an hour. After the girls entered the house, they each went into a different room. Each room contained something that scared the girls. Use the clues to determine which room each girl visited and what scared her. In the chart below, use checks to mark the room visited and the scary thing in it and Xs for the rest.

1. Camila went into the bedroom and was happy there were no ghosts in there.

2. Alma was too scared to go into the basement because she knew there was a mummy in there.

3. Bettina visited the kitchen and was glad she did not find any insects.

4. Danielle was scared by a mummy.

5. The person who visited the attic was scared by an eight-legged creature that fell from the ceiling.

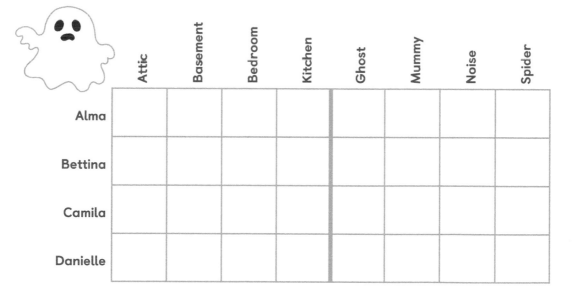

	Attic	Basement	Bedroom	Kitchen	Ghost	Mummy	Noise	Spider
Alma								
Bettina								
Camila								
Danielle								

RIDDLE ME THIS! Why are elephants always broke?

A DAY AT THE ADVENTURE PARK

Antonio, Bree, Cedric, and Della spent the day at a local adventure park. After playing together in the morning, they spent the afternoon doing their favorite activities: rock climbing, go-kart racing, playing miniature golf, and playing games at the arcade. Each child is wearing a different color T-shirt: red, yellow, green, or blue. Use the clues to determine the favorite activity and T-shirt color for each child. In the chart below, use checks to mark the favorite activity and the T-shirt color and Xs for the rest.

1. Bree played a game where she hit a ball with a club. The color of her T-shirt is yellow or green.

2. Cedric went rock climbing or played in the arcade.

3. Della loves race cars. She is wearing a green or blue T-shirt.

4. Antonio is afraid of heights.

5. The person who went to the arcade is wearing a blue T-shirt.

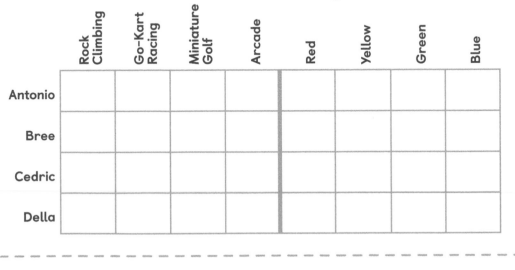

	Rock Climbing	Go-Kart Racing	Miniature Golf	Arcade	Red	Yellow	Green	Blue
Antonio								
Bree								
Cedric								
Della								

RIDDLE ME THIS! What did the clown say to his son when the boy told his dad he wanted to be a clown?

LUNCHTIME

At the school's picnic fundraiser in the park, each person got to choose a main dish and a dessert. Use the clues to determine what Angela, Brooklyn, Camden, and Deshan ordered. In the chart below, use checks to mark the main dish and dessert ordered and Xs for the rest.

1. Deshan does not like corn dogs or hot dogs.

2. The person who ordered the funnel cake also ordered the hot dog.

3. Camden's main dish and dessert start with the same letter as his name.

4. Angela did not order a funnel cake or cotton candy. She also likes sandwiches.

5. The person who ordered cheese pizza also ordered cotton candy.

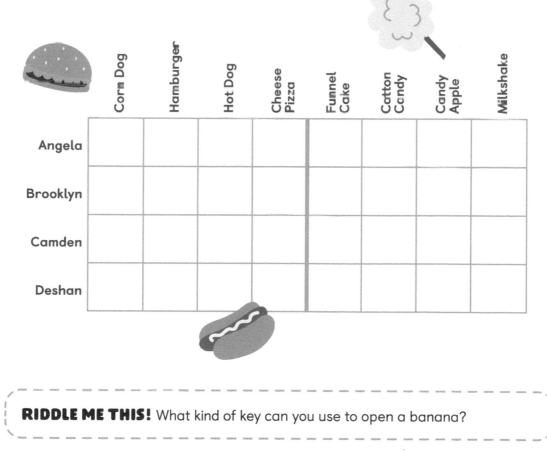

	Corn Dog	Hamburger	Hot Dog	Cheese Pizza	Funnel Cake	Cotton Candy	Candy Apple	Milkshake
Angela								
Brooklyn								
Camden								
Deshan								

RIDDLE ME THIS! What kind of key can you use to open a banana?

FUN AT THE SCHOOL CARNIVAL

Zora and her dad spent Saturday afternoon at the school carnival. During the first hour, she completed five activities and won a different prize after each activity. Use the clues to determine in what order she completed the activities and the prize she won at each activity. In the chart below, use checks to mark the order of the activities and the prize won for each activity and Xs for the rest.

1. The line for darts was long, so Zora waited for a while before getting in that line.

2. After the duck pond, Zora walked away with a new pet.

3. Zora and her dad went to the beanbag toss with empty hands but left with sunglasses.

4. Zora played bottle shoot right before the ring toss and right after the duck pond.

5. When Zora arrived at the ring toss, she had a goldfish, keychain, and pair of sunglasses. When she left, she also had a giant lollipop.

6. After the last activity, Zora received a teddy bear.

	1st	2nd	3rd	4th	5th	Giant Lollipop	Goldfish	Keychain	Stuffed Animal	Sun-glasses
Beanbag Toss										
Bottle Shoot										
Darts										
Duck Pond										
Ring Toss										

RIDDLE ME THIS! Where does a monkey go if he loses his tail?

FAMILY TIME WITH THE BROWNS

The Brown family spent the day at a local arcade. Each child in the Brown family is a different age and won a different number of tickets. Use the clues to determine each child's age and the number of tickets won. In the chart below, use checks to mark the child's age and number of tickets won and Xs for the rest.

1. None of the boys has an even number of tickets.

2. Noah collected more tickets than the girls.

3. The youngest child is a girl. She collected more tickets than her sister.

4. The oldest boy collected more tickets than Emma but less than Ava.

5. Emma is older than Noah but younger than Liam and Oliver.

	6 yo	7 yo	8 yo	9 yo	10 yo	49 tickets	64 tickets	75 tickets	96 tickets	101 tickets
Ava										
Emma										
Liam										
Noah										
Oliver										
49 tickets					
64 tickets					
75 tickets					
96 tickets					
101 tickets					

✳ **Hint:** Liam is not the oldest.

RIDDLE ME THIS! Why don't monkeys play games in the jungle?

PARTY TIME

Elijah celebrated his birthday at a local park with his friends. Before playing games, Elijah and his four friends measured their heights. At lunch, the five friends compared their birthdays and their heights. They were all born during the same year. Use the clues to determine each child's birthday and height. In the chart below, use checks to mark the child's birthday and height and Xs for the rest.

1. The person with the last birthday of the year is also the shortest.

2. Isabella is 1 inch taller than James.

3. Elijah's birthday is in the spring. There is one person taller than him.

4. The person who has a birthday in August is more than 54 inches tall.

5. The person who has a birthday in June is 55 inches tall.

6. Sophia is not taller than William.

	Feb 28	April 15	June 2	Aug 9	Dec 13	52 in	53 in	55 in	57 in	59 in
Elijah										
Isabella										
James										
Sophia										
William										
52 in					
53 in					
55 in					
57 in					
59 in					

✳ **Hint:** The difference between the height of the girls is 2.

RIDDLE ME THIS!
What made the clown sad?

CHAPTER 6

FACT-FINDING WITH DEDUCTION

INTRODUCTION

Deductive reasoning happens when we use clues to arrive at a conclusion. When you use deductive reasoning, you are building critical thinking and problem-solving skills. Scientists and mathematicians use deductive reasoning to draw conclusions and make generalizations that help us understand our world.

To use deductive reasoning to solve a problem, use the given clues or pictures to help you determine the answer.

Here's an example:

Which object is not like the others?

If we look at each picture, we can see they all contain a triangular-shaped object. When we look a little closer, we can conclude the cake, tent, and watermelon pictures have two triangles, but the pyramid has four triangles, one on each side. This is different from the other pictures, which only have two triangles.

It's your turn! Each problem gets a little harder than the one before. Use the hints to help you with the last two. Time to put your brain to work!

ODD ONE OUT

In each set of four pictures, circle the object that is the odd one out.

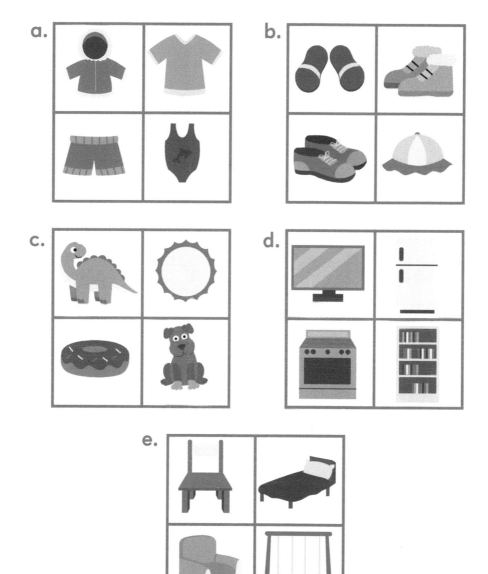

a.

b.

c.

d.

e.

RIDDLE ME THIS! Why couldn't the farmer keep a secret?

SHAPE LOGIC

In each set of four pictures, circle the object that does not belong.

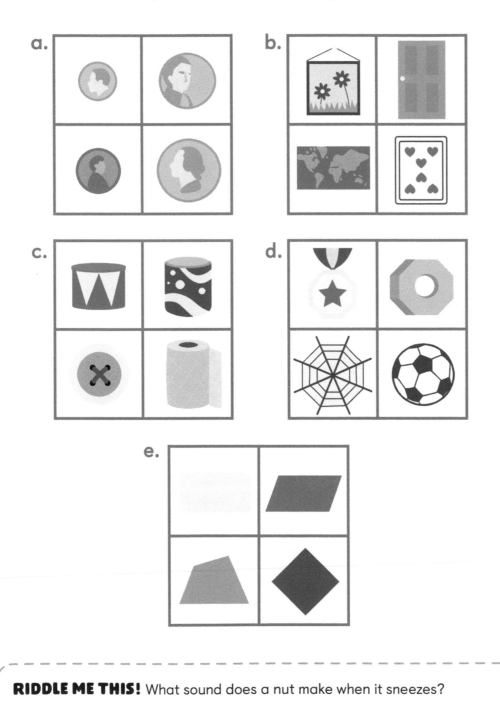

a.

b.

c.

d.

e.

RIDDLE ME THIS! What sound does a nut make when it sneezes?

ANIMAL LOGIC

Complete each statement below by filling in the blank.

a. If all insects have six legs, and a beetle is an insect, then a beetle _____.

b. If all birds lay eggs, and a flamingo is a bird, then a flamingo _____.

c. If all reptiles have special skin made of scales or bony plates, and a lizard is a reptile, then a lizard _____.

d. If all mammals have fur, and a zebra is a mammal, then a zebra _____.

e. If all fish are cold-blooded, and a shark is a fish, then a shark _____.

RIDDLE ME THIS! What did the nurse give to a sick lemon?

MATH LOGIC

Complete each statement below by filling in the blank.

a. If all triangles have three sides, and a yield sign is a triangle, then a yield sign _____.

b. If all quadrilaterals have four sides, and a kite is a quadrilateral, then a kite _____.

c. If all octagons have eight sides, and a stop sign is an octagon, then a stop sign _____.

d. If all cones have a circle at the bottom, and a tepee is shaped like a cone, then a tepee _____.

e. If all rectangles have two pairs of sides that are the same length and a square is a rectangle, then a square _____.

RIDDLE ME THIS! What has a lot of rings but no fingers?

HOW ARE THEY THE SAME?

What do the images in each group below have in common with one another? Based on your answer, add the fourth missing picture to each group.

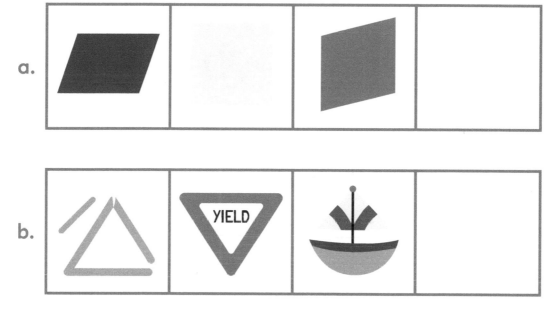

a.

b.

c.

RIDDLE ME THIS! Why did the mushroom get invited to the party?

NUMBER LOGIC

What do the numbers in each group below have in common with one another? Based on your answer, add the fourth missing number to each group.

a.

| 13 | 27 | 35 | |

b.

| 45 | 10 | 60 | |

c.

| 36 | 18 | 27 | |

RIDDLE ME THIS! How is a dog like a tree?

FRUITY SUMS

For each group below, use the clues to determine the value of each fruit. Then find the sum of the fruits in the last line.

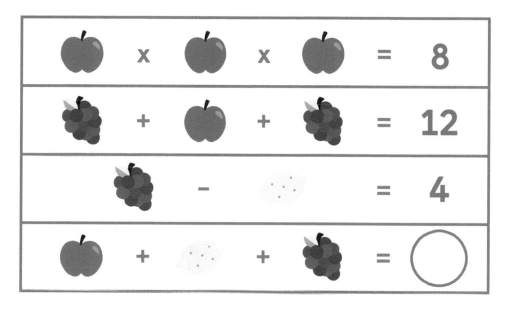

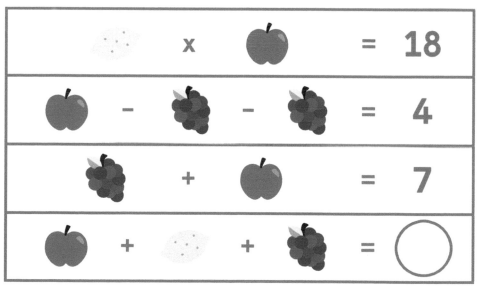

RIDDLE ME THIS! What plant gives the best kisses?

FIND THE SOLUTION

For each group below, use the clues to determine the value of each fruit. Then find an answer for the last line.

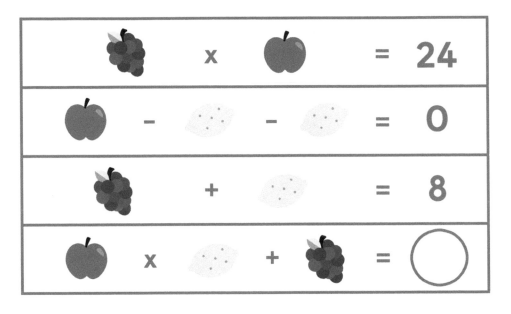

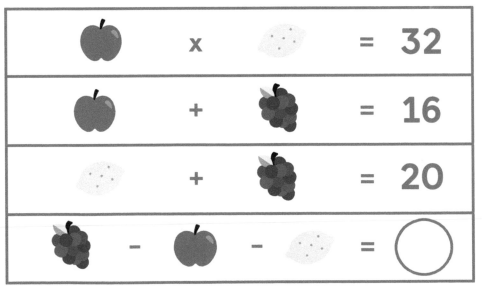

RIDDLE ME THIS! What happens when you plant a light bulb?

70   AWESOME LOGIC PUZZLES FOR KIDS

NATURE WALK

Read each word problem, and use the clues to determine the correct answer. Use the space below each problem to show your thinking.

a. Forest Ranger Ralph and his helpers estimate the number of animals that live in the forest he patrols. In the first area, they counted 9 fewer bears than porcupines and half as many porcupines as deer. If they counted 34 deer, how many animals did they count? _____

b. A local park has three campgrounds. The three campgrounds contain a total of 42 tents combined. Campground C has 7 fewer tents than Campground B. Campground A has 5 more tents than Campground C. How many tents are in each campground? _____

✳ **Hint:** Make sure the numbers you choose match all the clues.

RIDDLE ME THIS! What kind of tree is like a hand?

SIBLING FUN

Read each problem. Use the clues to determine the answer. Use the space below each problem to show your thinking.

a. Frank has two brothers, Brandon and Carter. The sum of the three brothers' ages is 64. Frank is older than Brandon, but Brandon is not the youngest. Carter is 17 years old. The difference between Brandon's age and Carter's age is 5. How old are Frank and Brandon? _____

b. Amara has two sisters, Nia and Zendaya. The sum of the three sisters' ages is 36. Zendaya is the youngest. Amara's age is double Zendaya's age. If Nia is 12 years old, how old are Amara and Zendaya? _____

❋ **Hint:** Make sure the ages match all the clues.

┌───┐
RIDDLE ME THIS! Why did the cucumber ask for help?
└───┘

PUZZLE ANSWERS

CHAPTER 1 PUZZLE ANSWER KEY

Double Dots

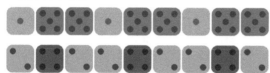

Making Patterns with Pawns

Fun with Spinners

Playing Card Patterns

The number of objects on each card follow a pattern: 1, 3, 5, 1, 3, 5, 1.

The colors on the cards follow a pattern: black, red, black, red, black, red, black.

The shapes on the cards follow a pattern: club, diamond, club, diamond, club, diamond, club.

The next card would be a red card with three diamonds.

Ready, Set, Tic-Tac-Toe

Dicey Patterns

Domino Patterns

Spinning Spinners

Fun with Dots and Dice

Seeing Spots

CHAPTER 2 PUZZLE ANSWER KEY

Lemonade Stand

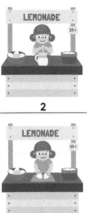

2

4

1

3

Rainy Weather

4

3

1

2

Skip Counting

You add 6 to the number on each shirt to get the number on the next shirt in the line. The "9" on the second shirt equals 3 + 6. To get the number for the third shirt, you add 6 to "9" from the second shirt, and 9 + 6 = 15. The "21" on the fourth shirt equals 15 + 6. To get the number for the fifth shirt, you add 6 to "21" from the fourth shirt, and 21 + 6 = 27.

Each shirt is 6 more than the previous shirt.

Number Sequences

Each shirt is 8 more than the previous shirt.

Hundreds Chart Pictures

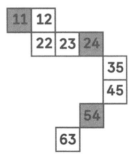

Find the Missing Numbers

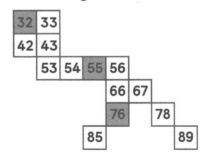

Intersecting Squares

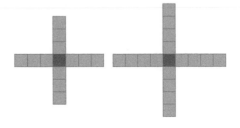

Tricky Triangles

Square Staircases

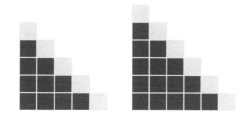

Growing Gardens

CHAPTER 3 PUZZLE ANSWER KEY

Looking at Lines

1. 4; 2. 12; 3. 4; 4. 8; 5. 4; 6. 10; 7. 3; 8. 0

Seeing in Black and White

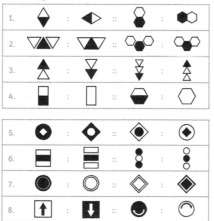

What's My Color?

1. orange; 2. yellow; 3. white; 4. blue;
5. green; 6. red; 7. red; 8. green

Special Characteristics

1. square; 2. four; 3. square; 4. night;
5. cold-blooded; 6. hands; 7. school; 8. sky

Cafeteria Fun

1. peanut butter; 2. lemonade;
3. pumpkin pie; 4. chocolate chip cookie
or any dessert with chocolate chips;
5. cheese pizza; 6. fish sticks;
7. spaghetti; 8. pancakes or waffles

Numbers Game

1. 35; 2. 54; 3. 12; 4. 35; 5. 90; 6. 35;
7. 21; 8. 22

Sports Spectacular

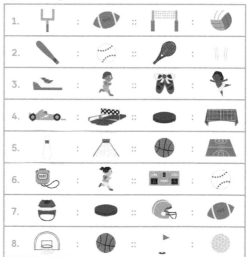

Where Do I Belong?

1. fruit; 2. bird; 3. insect; 4. dessert;
5. desert; 6. reptile; 7. science; 8. music

What's the Rule?

1. 40; 2. 16; 3. 60; 4. 100; 5. 8; 6. 50;
7. 150; 8. 100

Seeing Multiples

1. 10; 2. 9; 3. 80; 4. 11; 5. 72; 6. 10;
7. 49; 8. 7

CHAPTER 4 PUZZLE ANSWER KEY

Matchstick Houses

More or Less

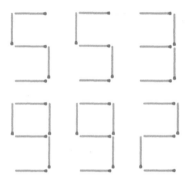

Starting with Squares

Nine More or Less

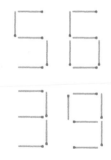

Transforming Triangles

Matchstick Equalities

$9 - 7 = 2$

$8 - 5 = 3$

Smallest to Largest

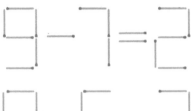

Balancing Equations

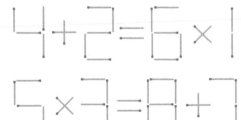

$4 + 2 = 6 \times 1$

$5 \times 3 = 8 + 7$

Seeing Squares

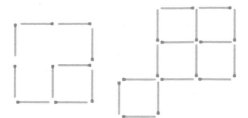

Making Words

CHAPTER 5 PUZZLE ANSWER KEY

A Trip to the Zoo
Angelo—Lion; Brooke—Penguin; Collin—Polar Bear; Donetta—Flamingo

Toy Department
Cheetahs—Right; Giraffes—Middle Left; Lions—Middle Right; Zebras—Left

The Reptile House
Turtles—Left Side; Iguanas—Middle Left; Snakes—Right Side; Komodo Dragon—Center; Crocodiles—Middle Right

Go-Kart Races
Arnav—Yellow; Bobby—Blue; Cam—Green; Diego—Red

Haunted Mansion
Alma—Attic/Spider; Bettina—Kitchen/Ghost; Camila—Bedroom/Noise; Danielle—Basement/Mummy

A Day at the Adventure Park
Antonio—Arcade/Blue; Bree—Miniature Golf/Yellow; Cedric—Rock Climbing/Red; Della—Go-Kart Racing/Green

Lunchtime
Angela—Hamburger/Milkshake; Brooklyn—Hot Dog/Funnel Cake; Camden—Corn Dog/Candy Apple; Deshan—Pizza/Cotton Candy

Fun at the School Carnival
Beanbag Toss—1st/Sunglasses; Bottle Shot—3rd/Keychain; Darts—5th/Stuffed Animal; Duck Pond—2nd/Goldfish; Ring Toss—4th/Giant Lollipop

Family Time with the Browns
Ava—6 years old/96 tickets; Emma—8 years old/64 tickets; Liam—9 years old/49 tickets; Noah—7 years old/101 tickets; Oliver—10 years old/75 tickets

Party Time
Elijah—April 15th/57 inches; Isabella—February 28th/53 inches; James—December 13th/52 inches; Sophia—June 2nd/55 inches; William—August 9th/59 inches

CHAPTER 6 PUZZLE ANSWER KEY

Odd One Out

a. The coat is the odd one out because it is worn in the winter. The other clothing items are not worn in the winter.

b. The hat is the odd one out because it is the only item that is not worn on your feet.

c. The sun is the odd one out because it is the only item that does not begin with the letter *D*.

d. The bookshelf is the odd one out because it is the only item that does not use electricity.

e. The swing set is the odd one out because it is the only item that belongs outside of the house, not inside.

Shape Logic

a. The penny does not belong because it is the only coin that is not gray or silver colored.

b. The artwork does not belong because it is the only object that is a square.

c. The button does not belong because it is flat.

d. The soccer ball does not belong because it has pentagons (shapes with five sides). The other shapes are octagons (shapes with eight sides).

e. The green shape does not belong because it does not have opposite sides that are the same length.

Animal Logic

a. If all insects have six legs, and a beetle is an insect, then a beetle <u>has six legs</u>.

b. If all birds lay eggs, and a flamingo is a bird, then a flamingo <u>lays eggs</u>.

c. If all reptiles have special skin made of scales or bony plates, and a lizard is a reptile, then a lizard <u>has special skin made of scales or bony plates</u>.

d. If all mammals have fur, and a zebra is a mammal, then a zebra <u>has fur</u>.

e. If all fish are cold-blooded, and a shark is a fish, then a shark is <u>cold-blooded</u>.

Math Logic

a. If all triangles have three sides, and a yield sign is a triangle, then a yield sign <u>has three sides</u>.

b. If all quadrilaterals have four sides, and a kite is a quadrilateral, then a kite <u>has four sides</u>.

c. If all octagons have eight sides, and a stop sign is an octagon, then a stop sign <u>has eight sides</u>.

d. If all cones have a circle at the bottom, and a tepee is shaped like a cone, then a tepee <u>has a circle at the bottom</u>.

e. If all rectangles have two pairs of sides that are the same length and a square is a rectangle, then a square <u>has two pairs of sides that are the same length</u>.

How Are They the Same?

a. Any four-sided figure can be added to this group.
b. Any triangular-shaped object can be added to this group.
c. Any cube-shaped object can be added to this group.

Number Logic

a. Any odd number can be added to this group.
b. Any multiple of five can be added to this group.
c. Any multiple of nine or two-digit number whose digits have a sum of nine can be added to this group.

Fruity Sums

a. The sum of the fruits in the last line equals 8, because the apple has a value of 2, the grapes have a value of 5, and the lemon has a value of 1.
b. The sum of the fruits in the last line equals 10, because the apple has a value of 6, the grapes have a value of 1, and the lemon has a value of 3.

Find the Solution

a. The last line equals 14, because the apple has a value of 4, the grapes have a value of 6, and the lemon has a value of 2.
b. The last line equals 0, because the apple has a value of 4, the grapes have a value of 12, and the lemon has a value of 8.

Nature Walk

a. Forest Ranger Ralph and his helpers counted 59 animals.
b. Campground A has 15 tents. Campground B has 17 tents. Campground C has 10 tents.

Sibling Fun

a. Brandon is 22 years old and Frank is 25 years old.
b. Amara is 16 years old and Zendaya is 8 years old.

RIDDLE ME THIS! ANSWERS

CHAPTER I RIDDLE ME THIS! ANSWERS

Double Dots
What is the saddest fruit?
Answer: blueberry

Making Patterns with Pawns
Which fruit can be used to sip a drink?
Answer: strawberry

Fun with Spinners
Which vegetable has ears but can't hear?
Answer: corn

Playing Card Patterns
Which vegetable do people cry over?
Answer: onion

Ready, Set, Tic-Tac-Toe
Which fruit cannot be alone?
Answer: pear

Dicey Patterns
Which vegetable never wins a competition?
Answer: beet

Domino Patterns
Which fruit makes people go crazy?
Answer: bananas

Spinning Spinners
What is a bee's favorite fruit?
Answer: honeydew

Fun with Dots and Dice
Which fruit is most like a chicken?
Answer: eggplant

Seeing Spots
Which vegetable has the best animal collection? **Answer:** zucchini

CHAPTER 2 RIDDLE ME THIS! ANSWERS

Lemonade Stand
What has two legs and catches flies?
Answer: A baseball player

Rainy Weather
What do you get when you cross a pig and a basketball player?
Answer: A ball hog

Skip Counting
Which kind of cat is the best at bowling?
Answer: An alley cat

Number Sequences
What soccer position does a ghost play?
Answer: A ghoulie

Hundreds Chart Pictures
What do a baseball team and cupcakes have in common?
Answer: They need a good batter.

Find the Missing Numbers
What animal makes the best baseball player? **Answer:** A bat

Intersecting Squares
Why did the football coach yell at the cashier? **Answer:** He wanted his quarter back.

Tricky Triangles
What do basketball players do to stay cool during a game? **Answer:** They sit next to the fans.

Square Staircases
What kind of sport uses a ball that has feet but no hands? **Answer:** Football

Growing Gardens
What is the hardest thing for a runner to catch? **Answer:** His breath

CHAPTER 3 RIDDLE ME THIS! ANSWERS

Looking at Lines
What does a farmer call a bull when he sleeps? **Answer:** A bulldozer

Seeing in Black and White
Why did the teddy bear skip lunch? **Answer:** Because he was stuffed.

What's My Color?
Why do fish like salt water? **Answer:** Because pepper makes them sneeze.

Special Characteristics
Where do polar bears go to vote during an election? **Answer:** The North Pole

Cafeteria Fun
What do porcupines say when they kiss? **Answer:** Ouch!

Numbers Game
Why are fish smarter than other animals? **Answer:** Because they live in schools.

Sports Spectacular
Which animal was caught cheating in school? **Answer:** The cheetah

Where Do I Belong?
Why do frogs have more lives than cats? **Answer:** Because they croak every night.

What's the Rule?
How do bees travel to school? **Answer:** In a school buzz

Seeing Multiples
What happened after a lion swallowed a clown? **Answer:** He felt funny.

CHAPTER 4 RIDDLE ME THIS! ANSWERS

Matchstick Houses
Why did Nose decide to skip school today? **Answer:** He was being picked on.

More or Less
What is the secret to making straight As in school? **Answer:** Use a ruler.

Starting with Squares
How did the music teacher get locked out of his classroom? **Answer:** He left his keys in the piano.

Nine More or Less

During the last debate, what did the pencil sharpener say to the pencil? **Answer:** You're going in circles. Get to the point.

Transforming Triangles

What kind of bait do librarians use to catch fish? **Answer:** Bookworms

Matchstick Equalities

What did Zero say to Eight? **Answer:** I like your belt.

Smallest to Largest

Why did the teacher put on her sunglasses? **Answer:** Because her pupils were so bright.

Balancing Equations

Why did the kitchen timer in the cafeteria run so slow? **Answer:** Because it went back for seconds.

Seeing Squares

What math tool is king of the classroom? **Answer:** The ruler

Making Words

What is an owl's favorite class at school? **Answer:** *Owl*-gebra

CHAPTER 5 RIDDLE ME THIS! ANSWERS

A Trip to the Zoo

What do we call a circus performer who can see in the dark? **Answer:** An acrobat

Toy Department

What happened to the human cannonball? **Answer:** He got fired.

The Reptile House

What happened when the clown made the magician mad? **Answer:** He pulled his hare out!

Go-Kart Races

What do you get when you call a clown three times? **Answer:** A three-ring circus.

Haunted Mansion

Why are elephants always broke? **Answer:** They work for peanuts.

A Day at the Adventure Park

What did the clown say to his son when he told his dad he wanted to be a clown? **Answer:** Those are big shoes to fill.

Lunchtime

What kind of key can you use to open a banana? **Answer:** A monkey

Fun at the School Carnival

Where does a monkey go if he loses his tail? **Answer:** To a retailer

Family Time with the Browns

Why don't monkeys play games in the jungle? **Answer:** There are too many cheetahs there.

Party Time

What made the clown sad? **Answer:** She broke her funny bone.

CHAPTER 6 RIDDLE ME THIS! ANSWERS

Odd One Out

Why couldn't the farmer keep a secret?

Answer: Because corn has ears and potatoes have eyes.

Shape Logic

What sound does a nut make when it sneezes? **Answer:** Ca-shew

Animal Logic

What did the nurse give to a sick lemon?

Answer: Lemon aid

Math Logic

What has a lot of rings but no fingers?

Answer: A tree

How Are They the Same?

Why did the mushroom get invited to the party? **Answer:** Because he's a fungi.

Number Logic

How is a dog like a tree?

Answer: They both have a lot of bark.

Fruity Sums

What plant gives the best kisses?

Answer: Tulips

Find the Solution

What happens when you plant a light bulb? **Answer:** You get a power plant.

Nature Walk

What kind of tree is like a hand?

Answer: A palm tree

Sibling Fun

Why did the cucumber ask for help?

Answer: He was in a pickle.

A NOTE TO PARENTS AND TEACHERS

Logical thinking is a way to make sense of a situation. When we think logically, we look for patterns or clues to arrive at a conclusion. Logical thinking is essential to help children build both critical thinking and problem-solving skills. These skills will not only help children achieve higher levels of success in the classroom, but they will also help them make decisions and draw conclusions outside of the classroom. The skills involved in solving logic puzzles and brain teasers will also prepare children for careers in math, science, and technology. Jobs in these fields involve collaboration to create products that solve problems and make our lives easier.

Each chapter in this book provides a different experience and requires a different way of thinking about the task. In the classroom, these puzzles make great math starters, enrichment tasks, and problem-solving challenges for math or literacy centers. Parents may find these puzzles useful for extra practice, family activities, or to keep children engaged when traveling. The best way to tackle the puzzles is to allow children to select the activities that most interest them and provide support and encouragement when they get stuck. Productive struggle is healthy and can be nurtured with a hint or a clue to move children in the right direction.

CHAPTER 1: PATTERNS IN OUR WORLD

This chapter includes a variety of visual patterns to cultivate pattern recognition. Children use their reasoning skills to determine what comes next in the pattern and then extend them.